CONTENTS

Words in the glossary appear in **bold** type the first time they are used in the text.

HEADING TO THE POLLS

Every four years, millions of Americans vote in the presidential **election**. They cast a vote for the person they think should lead the country for the next four years. Elections don't always go as expected. Throughout U.S. history, some elections have become more famous than others.

A LOOK AT U.S. ELECTIONS

FAMOUS PRESIDENTIAL ELECTIONS

BY KATHRYN WESGATE

Gareth Stevens PUBLISHING

CRASHCOURSE

Please visit our website, www.garethstevens.com. For a free color catalog of all our high-quality books, call toll free 1-800-542-2595 or fax 1-877-542-2596.

Cataloging-in-Publication Data
Names: Wesgate, Kathryn.
Title: Famous presidential elections / Kathryn Wesgate.
Description: New York : Gareth Stevens Publishing, 2021. | Series: A look at U.S. elections | Includes glossary and index.
Identifiers: ISBN 9781538259665 (pbk.) | ISBN 9781538259689 (library bound) | ISBN 9781538259672 (6 pack)
Subjects: LCSH: Presidents--United States--Election--Juvenile literature. | Elections--United States--Juvenile literature. | Electoral college--United States--Juvenile literature. | Voting--United States--Juvenile literature.
Classification: LCC JK529.W47 2021 | DDC 324.6'3--dc23

First Edition

Published in 2021 by
Gareth Stevens Publishing
111 East 14th Street, Suite 349
New York, NY 10003

Editor: Kate Mikoley

Photo credits: Cover, p. 1 Pool/Getty Images; series art kzww/Shutterstock.com; series art (newspaper) MaryValery/Shutterstock.com; p. 5 Tetra Images/Getty Images; p. 7 Hill Street Studios/DigitalVision/Getty Images; p. 9 (https://commons.wikimedia.org/wiki/File:George_Washington_1795.jpg) Wikimedia; pp. 11, 19, 20 Bettmann/Getty Images; p. 13 GraphicaArtis/Archive Photos/Getty Images; p. 15 Everett Historical/Shutterstock.com; p. 17 https://upload.wikimedia.org/wikipedia/commons/a/a0/Maryland%2C_Antietam%2C_President_Lincoln_on_the_Battlefield_-_NARA_-_533297.jpg; p. 18 https://commons.wikimedia.org/wiki/File:Horace_Greeley_restored.jpg; p. 21 W. Eugene Smith/The LIFE Picture Collection/Getty Images; pp. 23, 25 Brooks Kraft/Sygma/Getty Images; p. 27 https://en.wikipedia.org/wiki/File:President_Barack_Obama.jpg; p. 29 Drew Angerer/Getty Images News/Getty Images.

Printed in the United States of America

Make the Grade

When people go to vote, they're taking part in a popular vote. The person with the most votes from the people wins the popular vote.

THE ELECTORAL COLLEGE

The president is elected by the Electoral College. Each state has a number of votes, called electoral votes, based on how many people live there. Voters called electors make up the Electoral College. The popular vote decides which **political party's** electors are chosen to vote for their **candidate**.

Make the Grade

Today, there are 538 electoral votes. A candidate needs at least 270 to become president.

NO CONTEST FOR WASHINGTON

In 1789, electors from 10 of the 13 states voted for the first president. The other three states didn't vote. All 69 electors picked George Washington. He's still the only president to have ever been chosen **unanimously** by the Electoral College!

Make the Grade

Unlike people who run for office today, Washington didn't campaign, or try to get people to vote for him. In fact, some were unsure if he would even take the job!

In 1792, Washington won unanimously again and was elected to his second term, or period, as president. In 1796, he decided not to run again. This began a practice of presidents not seeking more than two terms—although it wasn't always followed.

Make the Grade

In 1940, Franklin D. Roosevelt became the first president elected to a third term. He was elected a fourth time in 1944. An official term limit was later set at two.

THE EXCITING ELECTION OF 1800

At first, the Electoral College was set up differently than it is today. Electors had two votes. The person with the most votes became president. Whoever came in second was vice president. There was a problem in 1800: Thomas Jefferson and Aaron Burr tied!

Make the Grade

The **House of Representatives** broke the tie. They elected Jefferson as the third U.S. president. Burr became vice president.

SPLITTING UP

In 1860, many members of the Democratic political party in the North didn't want **slavery** to spread. Democrats in the South did. As a result, the Democrats **nominated** two presidential candidates. With Democrats split, Republican candidate Abraham Lincoln easily won.

Make the Grade

After the 1860 election, it was clear the United States had two major, or leading, political parties: the Democrats and the Republicans. They're still the two major parties today.

Lincoln and his party were against slavery spreading to new parts of the nation. The South disagreed and seceded, or left the country. This led to the American Civil War, a war fought from 1861 to 1865 between the Northern and Southern states.

Make the Grade

The Civil War began about a month after Lincoln took office. The Northern states were called the Union and the Southern states were called the Confederacy.

A DEADLY ELECTION

Ulysses S. Grant won the election of 1872. Some would say it wasn't much of a fight since the other major candidate was dead before voting was over! Horace Greeley got 44 percent of the popular vote but died before the Electoral College voted.

HORACE GREELEY

Make the Grade

Also in 1872, the first woman ran for president. Victoria Woodhull wasn't nominated by a major party—and women couldn't vote yet—but she ran anyway!

FALSE ON THE FRONT PAGE

In 1948, many **predicted** Thomas Dewey would beat Harry Truman for the presidency. The *Chicago Daily Tribune* printed the next day's paper before all the votes were counted. A **headline** ran stating that Dewey had won. Truman really won!

THOMAS DEWEY

HARRY TRUMAN

Make the Grade

Truman took a famous picture with the paper's headline, but others got it wrong, too. *LIFE* magazine had already called Dewey "the next president of the United States."

EXAMINING AN ELECTION

The 2000 election was one of the closest ever. Republican George W. Bush was running against Democrat Al Gore. Commonly, the winner is known by the day after the election. This year, even a month later, people didn't know for sure who won!

AL GORE

Make the Grade

The results were so close that one state could make a difference. The votes in Florida had to be counted multiple times.

In Florida, voters punched holes in **ballots** to mark their choices. Part of the paper stayed connected to some ballots. People disagreed on if these votes counted. Finally, the Supreme Court stopped the recounts. Gore won the popular vote, but Bush won more electoral votes, winning the election.

GEORGE W. BUSH

Make the Grade

Because of the way the Electoral College works, a person can win the popular vote but lose the election. As of 2019, this has happened five times—in 1824, 1876, 1888, 2000, and 2016.

CHANGE IN 2008

In 2008, more than 130 million people cast their votes for the next president. The **voter turnout** was higher than it had been in 40 years. Even more historic, the country elected its first African American president, Barack Obama.

MAKE THE GRADE

Obama, a Democrat, won electoral votes in states, such as Florida, that had been won by Republicans in the past two presidential elections.

ELECTION OF 2016

In 2016, Hillary Clinton ran against Donald Trump. Clinton was the first woman in the United States to be a presidential candidate for a major political party. Though she lost, it was closer than any woman had been to becoming president.

Make the Grade

Clinton won the popular vote by more than 2.8 million votes. However, she only received 227 electoral votes, while Trump received 304.

KEY MOMENTS FROM FAMOUS ELECTIONS

1789
George Washington is elected unanimously as the first president.

1800
Thomas Jefferson and Aaron Burr tie for president.

1860
Abraham Lincoln is elected. The Democratic and Republican parties become known as the two main parties.

1861
The American Civil War begins after Southern states leave the country due to Lincoln's election.

1872
Presidential candidate Horace Greeley dies before electoral votes are in. Victoria Woodhull is the first woman to run for president.

1948
Harry Truman unexpectedly beats Thomas Dewey.

2000
George W. Bush beats Al Gore after multiple vote counts.

2008
The first African American president, Barack Obama, is elected.

2016
Hillary Clinton is the first woman to run for a major party.

GLOSSARY

ballot: a sheet of paper listing candidates' names and used for voting

candidate: a person who is running for office

election: the act of voting someone into a government position

headline: a title written in large print over a news story

House of Representatives: one part of Congress, which is the branch of the U.S. government that makes laws

nominate: to choose someone for a job or position

political party: a group of people with similar beliefs and ideas about government who work to have their members elected to government positions

predict: to guess what will happen in the future based on facts or knowledge

slavery: the state of being owned by another person and forced to work without pay

unanimously: agreed on by everyone

voter turnout: the percentage of those who can vote who actually vote in an election

FOR MORE INFORMATION

BOOKS

Krasner, Barbara. *A Timeline of Presidential Elections.* North Mankato, MN: Capstone Press, 2016.

Martin, Bobi. *What Are Elections?* New York, NY: Britannica Educational Publishing in association with Rosen Educational Services, 2016.

WEBSITES

Electoral College Fast Facts

history.house.gov/Institution/Electoral-College/Electoral-College/
Visit the House of Representatives website to learn more about the Electoral College.

Presidential Election Process

www.usa.gov/election
Watch a video and view an infographic to see the process for becoming president.

Publisher's note to educators and parents: Our editors have carefully reviewed these websites to ensure that they are suitable for students. Many websites change frequently, however, and we cannot guarantee that a site's future contents will continue to meet our high standards of quality and educational value. Be advised that students should be closely supervised whenever they access the Internet.

INDEX